MONEY MATTERS

A Classroom Economy

Adding and Subtracting Decimals

Dona Herweck Rice

Consultants

Lisa Ellick, M.A.
Math Specialist
Norfolk Public Schools

Pamela Estrada, M.S.Ed.
Teacher
Westminster School District

Paul Larson
Retired Teacher and Administrator

Publishing Credits

Rachelle Cracchiolo, M.S.Ed., *Publisher*
Conni Medina, M.A.Ed., *Managing Editor*
Dona Herweck Rice, *Series Developer*
Emily R. Smith, M.A.Ed., *Series Developer*
Diana Kenney, M.A.Ed., NBCT, *Content Director*
Stacy Monsman, M.A., *Editor*
Kevin Panter, *Graphic Designer*

Image Credits: All images from iStock and/or Shutterstock.

Library of Congress Cataloging-in-Publication Data

Names: Rice, Dona, author.
Title: Money matters : classroom economy / Dona Herweck Rice.
Description: Huntington Beach, CA : Teacher Created Materials, [2018] |
   Includes index.
Identifiers: LCCN 2017029059 (print) | LCCN 2017041111 (ebook) | ISBN
   9781425859664 (eBook) | ISBN 9781425858209 (pbk.)
Subjects: LCSH: Money--Juvenile literature. | Economics--Juvenile literature.
   | Finance, Personal--Juvenile literature. | Financial literacy--Juvenile
   literature.
Classification: LCC HG221.5 (ebook) | LCC HG221.5 .R53 2018 (print) | DDC
   332.024--dc23
LC record available at https://lccn.loc.gov/2017029059

Teacher Created Materials

5301 Oceanus Drive
Huntington Beach, CA 92649-1030
http://www.tcmpub.com

ISBN 978-1-4258-5820-9

© 2018 Teacher Created Materials, Inc.

Table of Contents

School Business

Mr. Capaldi's fifth grade classroom is always interesting. *At least, most of the time it is*, Dani thought to herself, remembering the morning's pop quiz. She hadn't been completely prepared for that one!

Dani Jones is one of thirty kids in Mr. Capaldi's class—or Mr. C, as his students call him. Each day, class is an adventure. Mr. C knows how to make things interesting, and he really encourages each of his students to take charge of his or her learning. That's just fine with Dani. And now she is ready to take charge in a big way!

Mr. C runs a classroom **economy**, or a business model, in which each student earns "C-notes" (classroom dollars) for jobs, effort, and behavior. They can also lose money through **fines** and **penalties**. And when Mr. C's classroom store is open, they can purchase some great things with their C-notes.

Dani has been doing well with her money all year. But she has her sights set on a new job—the biggest job of all. So far, she has been paper monitor, tech monitor, recycling monitor, and ambassador. But now she has her eye on the prize. She is ready to be classroom banker!

Mr. C explains the classroom economy.

Dani

Mr. C prepares his lesson plans.

Mr. C's Classroom Economy

When Mr. C became a teacher, he noticed that his students did not always have good **financial** sense. He wanted to change that. So, he decided to build a classroom economy. He had never managed one before, and he knew he had a few things to do to get ready.

First up, Mr. C thought about how the classroom and school day were run. What tasks did he as the teacher need to do for the students? And what tasks would be good to **delegate** to the class to give them a chance to lead? Mr. C knew that the more responsibility students had for how the class was run, the more they would feel that the class belonged to them. They would feel **invested** in the class and motivated to keep things running well.

Mr. C also knew that his most important job was instructing students. He needed to plan their lessons and evaluate their work. But students could do many of the other things that needed to be done. They could hand out papers, work technology, run errands, greet guests, and so much more. They could work together as a team to get things done.

Keeping whiteboards clean is a classroom job.

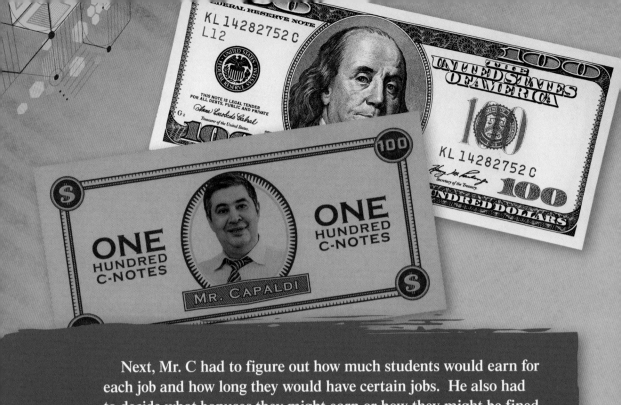

Next, Mr. C had to figure out how much students would earn for each job and how long they would have certain jobs. He also had to decide what bonuses they might earn or how they might be fined for neglect or errors made. The classroom economy would include money earned, money charged, and money spent. Mr. C needed a plan for all of it.

The next step was to prepare the materials. He designed his classroom dollar and called it a C-note. C-note is an old slang term for a $100 bill. The *c* comes from the Latin word *centum*, meaning "100." Mr. C thought that calling his money a C-note—*C* for *Capaldi*, *c* for *centum*—was a pretty good **pun**.

bank book

Mr. C also created bankbooks for students, so they could tally their income and **expenses**. They would be responsible for keeping track of their money. And they had to be sure that their figures matched the banker's calculations.

Lastly, Mr. C needed to gather items students could purchase with their C-notes. He had to assign each item a value. Mr. C thought students would like to buy useful things, such as pencils, erasers, and folders. He also thought they would like fun items, such as origami paper, stickers, and key chains.

LET'S EXPLORE MATH

Mr. C sometimes awards C-notes that do not have whole number values. Mr. C gave Oliver 10.35 C-notes, and Malik 10.53 C-notes. Oliver believes his C-notes are worth more than Malik's. Explain why he is incorrect, and how the values are different.

Credit

Mr. C explains that credit is a loan that must be paid back.

CREDIT CARD APPLICATION

		(First)		(State)	(Zip)	(Middle Initial)	Home Telephone ( ) -
Personal Information			(City)				Other Telephone ( ) -
Name (Last)							
Address (Mailing Address)							
E-Mail Address							

Current Income

...ate Or General Education (GED) Test Passed? Yes No

...recent first)

Earned

Degree
...ar

Ma...
or S...

The Class Meets the Economy

Dani and her classmates are Mr. C's most recent group of students. He has been using his classroom economy for 15 years. It is a **well-oiled machine** at this point. The class started using the system on the first day of school.

At first, Mr. C explained what a classroom economy is. He told the class about finances and that they would have to manage their own throughout their lives. Good financial sense could make all the difference in leading a **prosperous** life. A person should stay aware of income, expenses, and daily spending. Not paying attention to money can get a person in trouble.

One of the biggest lessons the class learned was that money going out should never be more than money coming in. That seems like common sense! But Mr. C said it is a common problem. Some people get into trouble with **credit**. They buy things they cannot afford and have expenses that exceed their earnings. Mr. C explained that challenges in life could make finances very difficult as well. But he also said that financial knowledge equals financial power.

Mr. C explained that the classroom would be organized by jobs. Students would complete an application for a job, telling why he or she should have that job. Mr. C conducted job interviews and hired students for the jobs. Jobs would be paid in C-notes each week and held for set lengths of time. One-week jobs were the easiest jobs with the simplest training. They paid on the lower end of the pay scale. Some jobs were one-month jobs. They required more complicated training and paid on the higher end of the pay scale.

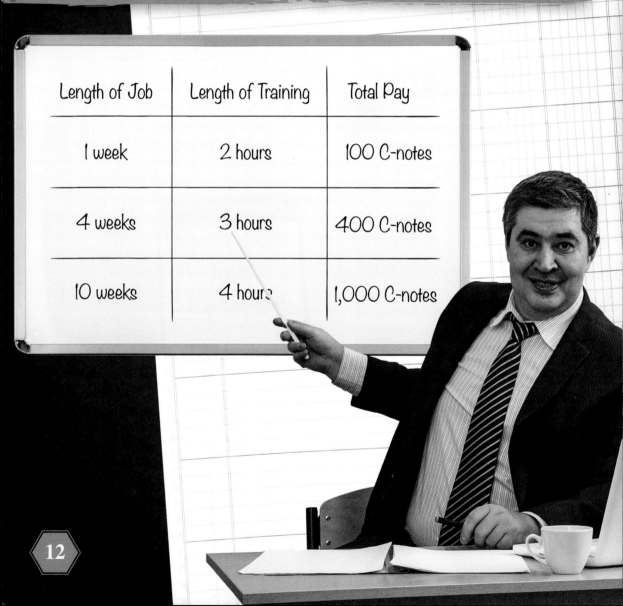

Length of Job	Length of Training	Total Pay
1 week	2 hours	100 C-notes
4 weeks	3 hours	400 C-notes
10 weeks	4 hours	1,000 C-notes

Bank Accounts for Mr. Capaldi's class

	Initials	Date
Prepared By		
Approved By		

October – Week 2

Date	Student/ Transaction	Deposit +	Withdrawal –	Balance =
	Dani Jones:	100		
10/6	paycheck		25	
10/6	folder and pencil set			75
10/8				
	Cesar Romero:	200		
10/7	paycheck	50		
10/8	behavior reward			250
10/8				
	Malik Johnson:	50		50
10/4	paycheck			
10/8				
	Oliver Mitchell:	100		
10/6	paycheck		20	
10/7	tardy fine			80
10/8				

The banker is the most challenging job of all. It is a 10-week job, so only four students a year serve as banker. It pays the most of all the jobs, but it also has the most responsibility and training. The banker pays each student on Friday for that week's work. The banker also tracks each person's income and classroom expenses. Expenses are paid at the classroom shop. The shop is open every Monday and Wednesday afternoon for 20 minutes. The shopkeeper runs the shop, but the banker manages its **books** and keeps track of each student's purchases.

Throughout the week, students also might receive penalties or fines. These are for late assignments, tardiness, damaged classroom materials, classroom disruptions, and other behaviors that cost the class time. ("Time is money!" Mr. C says.) Mr. C makes decisions about fines and gives them to the student and the banker to calculate.

Each student has one more big expense. Every student has **rent** to pay! Rent is charged at the beginning of every month. Each student pays rent for his or her desk and desk maintenance. If the student damages the desk in any way, his or her monthly rent will increase. You can bet that students are always extra careful to keep their desks in good repair. No one writes or carves on their desks!

To begin the classroom economy, each student receives a special gift. They each get a bonus just for being a student in Mr. C's class! The bonus is a true C-note: one hundred of Mr. C's classroom dollars. With the bonus, students are able to begin paying rent right away. Mr. C is sure to point out that things usually do not work that way in the world outside the classroom! Money is not usually just given to a person for showing up.

Mr. C's Classroom Fine Ticket

☐	Tardy 4.50 C-notes	☐	Chewing Gum 0.75 C-notes
☐	Unprepared 10 C-notes	☐	Disrespectful 5 C-notes
☐	Bullying 100 C-notes	☐	Note Passing 3.75 C-notes
☐	Wearing Hat 2.50 C-notes	☐	No Homework 1.25 C-notes

Suppose Dani earns 8 C-notes for good behavior. Later that day, she is fined 2.50 C-notes for forgetting to remove her hat. How many C-notes does Dani have left after paying the fine? Use the model to find and prove your solution.

Dani's Economic Journey

When Dani became a student in Mr. C's class, she received her bankbook and **deposit** of 100 C-notes to begin. She felt rich! Monthly desk rent in Mr. C's class is 25 C-notes, so Dani paid that right away. She marked 100 in her bankbook and subtracted 25 for the rent. That left her with 75 C-notes to begin the school year. Dani thought about her expenses for the rest of the year. If she did not make any more money, she could pay three months rent but nothing after that. She would also have no money for any other expenses. Dani set her sights on getting a classroom job right away!

Mr. C explained what each job entailed, and Dani listened carefully. She wanted to begin to build her savings. Mr. C said that paper monitors handed out and collected all classroom papers. There would be two paper monitors. If she got the job, she could easily get to know the names of all her classmates. Plus, the job paid 10 C-notes for one week of work. Dani decided to apply for paper monitor. Mr. C conducted interviews for all the jobs. Four students applied for paper monitor, but Dani and a boy named Cesar got the jobs!

Cesar

Dani

Dani and Cesar work as paper monitors in their classroom to earn C-notes. They decide to save some of their earnings, but spend some on items that they want or need. Use a number line similar to the one shown below to find and prove your solutions.

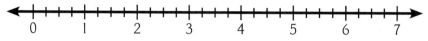

1. Dani buys a package of stickers for 2.25 C-notes and a notebook for 4.50 C-notes. How much does she spend?

2. Cesar buys an eraser and a key chain for 5.75 C-notes. The eraser costs 1.25 C-notes. How much is the key chain?

You're hired! Welcome to the team, paper monitors.

Dani completes a digital application to be tech monitor.

Dani loved her first job. She loved it so much that she applied for it again! But Mr. C said it was important that different students get a chance for each job. That seemed fair. And Dani really wanted a job she could hold onto for a longer amount of time. She also wanted to put a little more money in her savings account.

She decided to try for a month-long job, but she would have to wait three weeks for one to become available. She knew the one she wanted. Mr. C had explained the job of tech monitor, and Dani was **intrigued**. The tech monitor ran the electronic equipment for the class. He or she also made sure that all electronics were in good working order each day and turned off at the end of the day. That was a lot of responsibility, but Dani loved working with electronics. She decided to go for it.

In her interview, Dani explained to Mr. C how she and her dad had built a radio at home. She had also uploaded all her apps on her home computer herself. She **assured** him that she would take the responsibility seriously. Dani must have convinced Mr. C, because she got the job! She would be class tech monitor for one month. Best of all, she would earn 50 C-notes!

LET'S EXPLORE MATH

Dani earns 12.50 C-notes for one week as tech monitor.

1. That week, Dani spends 3.55 C-notes on a new folder. How much does she have left?

2. Suppose Mr. C subtracts 2.45 C-notes for each day students are absent from school and cannot do their classroom jobs. Dani is out sick for two days after buying the folder. How much does she have left?

Class tech monitor was a tough job with a lot of responsibility, but Dani did it well. She added the 50 C-notes she earned to her bankbook, just as she had added 10 from her paper monitor job. She also subtracted three expenses. One morning, she overslept and was five minutes late to school. She was marked tardy and got a 4.50 C-note fine. She would never do that again! Dani had also purchased 15 C-notes worth of goods at the class shop one day and 10 another day. She was happy with her purchases but wanted to earn some money to build her savings.

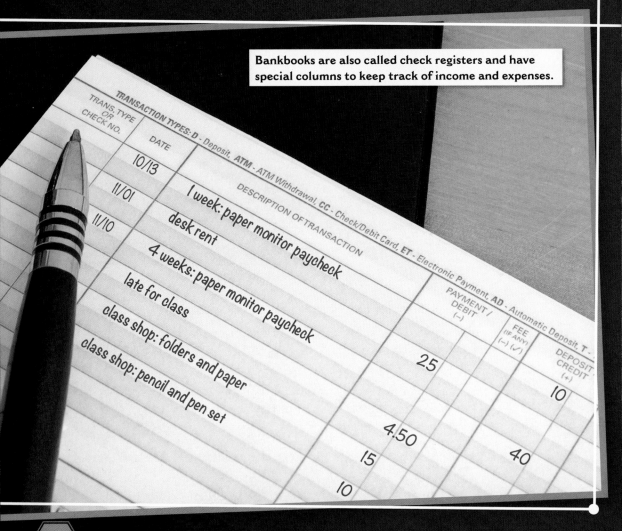

Bankbooks are also called check registers and have special columns to keep track of income and expenses.

TRANS. TYPE OR CHECK NO.	DATE	TRANSACTION TYPES: D - Deposit, ATM - ATM Withdrawal, CC - Check/Debit Card, ET - Electronic Payment, AD - Automatic Deposit, T - DESCRIPTION OF TRANSACTION	PAYMENT/ DEBIT (−)	FEE (IF ANY) (−) (✓)	DEPOSIT CREDIT (+)
	10/13	1 week: paper monitor paycheck			10
	11/01	desk rent	25		
	11/10	4 weeks: paper monitor paycheck			40
		late for class	4.50		
		class shop: folders and paper	15		
		class shop: pencil and pen set	10		

Many schools recycle.

Dani was also very busy these days. She decided to apply for a job with less responsibility than tech monitor. Recycling monitor sounded about right. All she had to do was collect the class's recyclables after lunch each day. Then, on Friday, she would deliver them to Mr. Cooper, the school custodian. He took all of the school's recycling to a recycling center in town. It was a good program, and Dani was happy to be a part of it. She applied, and once again, she got the job.

The recycling job went well, and Dani was glad to add 5 C-notes to her bankbook. Even so, she wanted to make more money than that.

She decided to apply for a higher paying job. Class ambassador sounded intriguing. The ambassador greeted visitors to the classroom and made sure they had everything they needed. More importantly, the ambassador helped new students in the class and grade level. He or she also watched out for any students who seemed to be left out and alone. Mr. C made it clear that their school was a no-bully zone for everyone. Even so, the ambassador made extra sure that everyone felt safe and welcome. That was something Dani could really get behind! She had only been going to this school since September, and she knew how hard it could be to fit in. As ambassador, she would help others feel included.

Dani was very excited about the job. She applied and was truly happy to hear that she got it! It would be a win-win: she could help others, and she would also earn 50 C-notes. Dani decided this just might be the best job of all.

LET'S EXPLORE MATH

Dani is helping the new student, Milo, understand Mr. C's classroom economy.

1. Milo earns 2.70 C-notes each day. After two days, does he earn more or less than 5 C-notes? How do you know?

2. Suppose Mr. C increases Milo's pay by 0.90 C-notes each day. Will he earn more or less than 3.70 C-notes each day? How do you know?

Dani welcomes a new student to the class.

Class Ambassador

As ambassador, Dani made new friends. When the month was over, she decided to keep being an ambassador on her own. She felt good helping others, and she gained much more than money.

For the next few weeks, Dani tried other jobs as well. She earned 10 C-notes as agenda monitor, writing the class assignments on the board. She earned 5 C-notes as light monitor and 10 as errand runner. But all the while, Dani had her eyes on a really big job. It required a lot of time and responsibility, but she knew she could handle it. She decided to apply for banker. Dani showed Mr. C how carefully she kept her own bankbook and reminded him of her **precision** when completing math tasks. She assured him she could do the job and asked for a chance to prove herself. Mr. C hired her on the spot. He said he knew she could do it and had been waiting for her to apply!

Dani loved being the banker and even thought it might be a good job in her future. Best of all, she earned 100 C-notes for a job well done!

Dani writes the homework assignments on the board.

Mr. C inspects Dani's math tasks.

LET'S EXPLORE MATH

Pretend you are a student in Mr C's class. Balance your bankbook.
Use addition and subtraction to find your final balance.

Description	+ / −	Amount
Starting balance		212.54
Monthly rent	_____	25.00
Balance:		_____
Paycheck	_____	15.75
Balance:		_____
Good behavior reward	_____	8.00
Balance:		_____
Origami paper purchase	_____	13.30
Final Balance:		_____

Classroom Economy for the Win!

Dani finished the school year 55 C-notes **in the black**. Since her C-notes expired at the end of the year, she went on a shopping spree at the class shop. But she kept one C-note as a **souvenir**. Dani wanted it as a reminder of all she had learned in Mr. C's interesting, challenging, and **profitable** class!

On the last day of school, Mr. C and the class talked about their classroom economy. They discussed the good and bad choices they made when it came to money. They discussed the importance of preparing for a job and doing it well. Students also saw that the more aware they were of their income and expenses, the better off they were in the long run.

Most of the class wanted to continue the classroom economy the next year. They decided to tell their new teacher all about it and see if they could set it up themselves. Mr. C said he would be their advisor if they did! Dani hoped she would get a chance to be banker again. She knew that with a deposit of hard work and common "cents," she would make a valuable contribution to her future—one that would pay off for years to come!

Mr. C is pleased that his students learned the value of a dollar...or a C-note!

🔩⚙️ Problem Solving

Dani and Robyn are not only classmates but also teammates on the school's soccer team. The soccer team is planning to see a professional match. Dani and Robyn want to raise money to help pay for tickets. They decide to use what they learned in Mr. C's classroom economy to create a business. They will bake energy bars and sell them to other players at practice.

Dani and Robyn choose a recipe and think about supplies. The energy bars have several ingredients. Luckily, Robyn's parents donate salt, cinnamon, olive oil, and honey. The girls will need to buy the other ingredients at the grocery store. They do some price research online and write a shopping list. Dani's older brother agrees to give them an interest-free loan for the ingredients and a ride to the grocery store. Now, Dani and Robyn need a business plan. Use the shopping list to help them create it.

1. How much money will Dani's brother need to loan her and Robyn for ingredients?

2. One batch of the recipe makes 20 energy bars. What is the lowest cost per bar that will cover the cost of ingredients?

3. Suppose Dani and Robyn email you for some business advice. They want to know:

   - what to charge for each bar to make a **profit**

   - the profit for each bar

   - the profit for 20 bars

Shopping List

rolled oats	$4.25
shredded coconut	$4.15
dried cherries	$18.70
chocolate chips	$3.25
sunflower seed butter	$9.65

Glossary

assured—expressed confidence

books—financial records

credit—money a bank lets someone use and pay back over time with interest added

delegate—to assign a task one usually does to someone else

deposit—amount of money put into a bank account

economy—the process or system by which goods and services are produced, sold, and bought

expenses—money spent regularly to pay for things

financial—having to do with money

fines—money paid for breaking a rule

in the black—having a profit

intrigued—interested

invested—having given time, money, or energy to make something better

penalties—punishments for errors or wrongdoings

precision—exactness

profit—money made after all costs and expenses are paid

profitable—bringing value (in this instance, a pun on financial profitability, or making money)

prosperous—having success with money

pun—joke made through wordplay

rent—amount paid to use a space for a set amount of time

souvenir—keepsake to remember something by

well-oiled machine—well-run operation

Index

Let's Explore Math

page 9:

Oliver is incorrect because although both students earned 10 whole C-notes, the decimal values are different. Oliver earned 35 hundredths of a C-note and Malik earned 53 hundredths of a C-note. So, Malik's C-notes are worth more than Oliver's by 18 hundredths (0.18)

page 15:

5.50 C-notes; Models should show two whole rectangles crossed out and 5 tenths of a rectangle crossed out.

page 17:

1. 6.75 C-notes; Number lines will vary. Example:

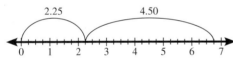

2. 4.50 C-notes; Number lines will vary. Example:

page 19:

1. 8.95 C-notes

2. 4.05 C-notes

page 22:

1. More than 5 C-notes; Explanations will vary, but may include that since 2.70 C-notes is more than 2.50 C-notes, the earnings must be more than 5 C-notes.

2. Less than 3.70 C-notes; Explanations will vary, but may include that since the pay is increased by less than 1 C-note, the new amount cannot be a whole C-note more.

page 25:

− ; 187.54; + ; 203.29; + ; 211.29; − ; 197.99

Problem Solving

1. $40.00

2. $2.00

3. Emails will vary, but should include a price per bar over $2.00, the amount of profit for each bar, and the amount of profit for 20 bars.